GETTING TO KNOW

Mykonos
& Delos

Contents

INTRODUCTION 10

GETTING TO KNOW 12

MYTH AND HISTORY 14

THE PORT 20

THE HORA 28

THE PARAPORTIANI 36

LITTLE VENICE 44

WINDMILLS 52

SIGHTSEEING 56

THE REST OF THE ISLAND 64

DELOS 72

INFORMATION 92

Introduction

Grey, blue, white:
Mykonos in three colours and four scenes.
The white houses, dazzling in the sunlight, with balconies and
stairways festooned with bright geraniums and pots of basil.
One facade blending into another, narrow flagstone alleys
winding among them and countless tiny churches topped with
blue and red domes. The white silhouettes of the windmills on
the hills above are a reminder of days gone by.
The maquis and the grey rock. Its monotony broken by the
outline of the prickly pear and the white houses, which seem to
jut straight from their bowels, their backs hunkered down
against the relentless north wind. Near the sea this grey mass
turns to gold sand before being covered by crystal clear water.
Or else it is shaped into dry stone walls that snake their way
around the island.
The whiter than white chapels raised on outcroppings so
forbidding one wonders how man ever
managed to set foot there.
The twisted trunks of trees in spots where the earth offers a bit
of shelter from the winds that whip through the island.
And all around, the blue of the sea, freshness and charm.
Sometimes inviting, sometimes threatening, the all-embracing
sea is the source of the island's wealth.

Getting to Know Mykonos

But let's take a closer look at Mykonos and try to get to know it better.

A barren, rocky island, it lies about 94 nautical miles from Piraeus, southeast of Tinos and north of Paros and Naxos. It belongs to the Cyclades group of islands and has an area of 85 sq. km. Its highest peaks, which do not exceed 350 m., are Prophitis Ilias Vorniotis and Prophitis Ilias Anomeritis. There is little vegetation and very few trees due to the composition of the soil and to its location in one of the windiest regions in Greece. Below the ground are rich lodes of lead, silver and barite.

The island possesses numerous sandy, sheltered beaches. All of them lie in the south of the island (Agios Ioannis, Ornos, Psarou, Platys Yialos, Paranga, Paradise, Super Paradise, Agrari, Elia, Kalo Livadi, Agia Anna, Kalafatis), the only exceptions being Ftelia and Panormos facing north and Agios Stefanos in the west. In earlier times, the islanders were fishermen and farmers.

Apart from fishing, they also worked in shipping and in shipbuilding and repairs. Those who lived from the land cultivated vines and vegetables. In the early 18th century they produced about 30,000 barrels of wine each year; its quality was said to be exceptional.

A considerable amount of wheat was also produced, and as we shall see in another chapter, exploitation of the winds that blow in the Cyclades gave rise to professions such as those of the miller and the baker which helped attract money to the island. Cattle and pigs were and still are raised on Mykonos; its beef though limited in quantity is considered delicious, while its sausages are famed throughout Greece.

In the past 40 years, tourism has upset the traditional rhythm of life in Mykonos. The locals have begun to devote their skills solely to jobs related to the industry — hotels, restaurants, travel agencies, etc. Once one of Greece's poorest islands, Mykonos was the first of the Cyclades to gain world fame. Today it continues to be the star of the Aegean.

Its attributes are the sun (some 3,000 hours of sunshine per year), the sparkling sea, golden sands and its traditional, quintessentially Cycladic architecture.

Myth and History

Now a bit about the history of the island. Although in the 20th century Mykonos has become the muse of numerous artists with admirers the world over, its role in history has been marginal. Despite the strategic importance of its location at the centre of the Aegean, its lack of fertile soil and water discouraged would-be colonists from settling and would-be conquerors from claiming it. Thus, its history is brief and little different from the rest of the Cyclades, with a few bright spots in the 18th and 19th century, chiefly due to its contribution to the Revolution of 1821. But first let's see how Mykonos got its name.

As with many other Greek place names, we must look to mythology.

It seems that the original Mykonos was the son of Anios, himself a son of Apollo. In other words, it was an island of light, taking its name from a hero closely related to the light- giving god. And the grey, glossy, granite rocks jutting from its soil also have a mythical connection. Legend has it that they were catapulted by Poseidon in a war against the giants.

Historical sources, however, are very few. Nevertheless, it is likely that the Lelegians or Carians were the first tribes to inhabit Mykonos. They seem to have been followed by the Egyptians, Phoenicians, Cretans and around 1000 B.C. by the Ionians. Skylax mentions that in the time of the Persian king Darius, there were at least two settlements on Mykonos. In our own era, traces of a prehistoric Cycladic civilization have been located in the vicinity of the Hora's Kastro and at Linos can be seen the ruins of two towers and sections of wall dating to the Classical period.

From antiquity the Mykonians must have been seafarers and farmers who were accustomed to living scattered about the island, as they do today.

In the historical era they must have worshipped Poseidon and Apollo, gods who were directly linked with the island's natural resources, the sea and the sun. Dionysos appears also to have been

▶ The fishermen spend a large part of their day patching their nets.

accorded special honour, while Demeter was worshipped as the protectress of agriculture.

In 478 B.C. the First Athenian Confederacy was founded and Mykonos was a charter member. Judging from the low taxes it paid, the economic conditions on the island cannot have been very prosperous. The proclamation of Delos as a free port in 166 B.C. brought greater prosperity to the area, from which Mykonos benefitted, too. When in 88 B.C., Delos was sacked by Mithridates, Mykonos fell into decline. During the Byzantine era it was a part of the province of Achaia and subsequently belonged to the Theme of the Aegean.

After the conquest of Constantinople by the Franks in 1204, the Venetians led by Marco Sanudo became lords of the Cyclades, while the government of Mykonos was ceded as a fief to the Ghisi family in whose hands it remained until the death of Giorgio Ghisi III in 1390. After that the island reverted to direct Venetian rule.

In 1537 it was devastated by Khaireddin Barbarossa, the Barbary pirate who became a Turkish admiral, and in the same year was subjugated by the Turks. From the mid 15th century and even during the Turkish domination, Mykonos was governed by "captains".

In 1615 after the death of the last captain, the people and the clergy of Mykonos held a meeting in the church of Prophitis Ilias outside the castle to elect two citizens to serve in his place for a term of one year. In this way, Mykonos public life was founded, developing according to the needs of the day, the privileges awarded by the Pashas, and their growing commercial activities. Thus the island was administered by two representatives of the people who were elected by universal vote on March 1st every year. Its economy was based on the production of cotton and excellent wine, which was supplied to the Venetian army of the Morea (Peloponnese).

From the start of the 16th century to the end of the 17th, Mykonos was a den for pirates and smugglers.

The islanders collaborated with the pirates, buying their booty at low prices and selling it in turn in Constantinople,

▲ Time for a chat. About what? The sea, of course.
► View of the port. Up above, exposed to the four winds, stand the windmills.

Italy and France. Their talent for commerce brought prosperity to Mykonos.

In 1545 Mykonos reverted for a short time to the Venetians, something which occurred also between 1645-1669 and 1684-1699.

However, internal strife in the Ottoman Empire, the Turco-Venetian wars, the slaughter and sacking of Greek settlements caused the population to dwindle dramatically. From 1633 to 1667 the island was virtually deserted, while in 1678 its few remaining inhabitants were decimated by an outbreak of plague.

From 1770 to 1774, the island fell under the domination of the Russians. The 18th century also saw an economic revival. Mykonos became a way-station for French ships bound for Smyrna and Constantinople. In the meantime, its own fleet was growing; by the start of the 18th century it numbered 50 caiques and 100 larger ships. Of the island's total population of 3,000, some 500 were sailors. It acquired a small shipyard and during the wars between the English and the French and the

ensuing blockades, the Mykonians managed to supply wheat to those cut off. The growth of shipping was accompanied by the development of cottage industries — with the women making cotton and woollen goods in their homes, breadmaking and the grinding of wheat into flour.

Thus the period between 1750 and 1815 was for Mykonos a time of great prosperity. During the War of Independence (1821), Mykonos did not remain aloof. On the contrary, numerous Mykonians led by their famous woman admiral Manto Mavroyenous, took an active role in the struggle.

By the middle of the 19th century, the rise of the steamboat and the inability of the islanders to adjust to the new trends caused the economy to shrink drastically. The Mykonians began to emigrate to other regions in search of a better life and continued to do so until the 1950s, when the first tourists coming came to pay homage to the antiquities at Delos discovered the magic of Mykonos, and a new chapter in the history of this small island opened.

The florist is a peddler, and so is the greengrocer, who has loaded his wares on the picturesque donkey, which casts a wondering eye at the specialties displayed in the restaurant.

The Port

As the ship approaches the island, those on board begin to take notice of the constantly changing landscape. Nature starts to work on their emotions. The awe induced by the steep rocks and the frenzied crashing of the waves over them gives way to the calm conjured up by the sight of a serene beach. And the changes continue up to the moment that the ship enters the harbour. On one side wild waves break against the walls of the houses of Alevkandra and on the other the silent presence of the windmills, white and still, immobilizes the passengers for an instant before they disembark. The crowds on the waterfront, colourful and noisy, are somehow an integral part of the whole scene. Their presence conveys from the first instant of arrival what makes Mykonos so special: the perfect harmonization of nature and man, which has permitted the survival of the inhabitants and the proper development of the island.

One glance at the Hora of Mykonos is enough for the visitor to spot the difference between it and other Cycladic towns. The Hora or capital is situated on the west coast of the island, between the bays of Agios Stefanos and Tourlos to the north and the peninsula of Agios Ioannis or Diakoftis, Korfos and Ornos to the south. In contrast with other Cycladic towns, most of which are built amphitheatrically on the slopes of hills or mountains, Mykonos has been laid out on flat ground, except for the low rise on which the Kastro — the medieval citadel — stands.

The visitor's first glimpse of Mykonos imprints itself forever on the memory: an image sculpted in relief from the extraordinary whiteness of its two-story cube-like buildings, interspersed with the coloured domes of the churches, the windmills standing sentinel on all the ridges of town, and the towering eminence of the Panayia Paraportiani, Mykonos's most famous church.

The port of Mykonos is the heart of the Hora. It is here that nearly all the island's business and social life take place, seemingly round the clock. Many of the town's most noteworthy sights also are located here.

The port has its own rhythm, every hour of the day and night, its dedicated

patrons, the fishermen, sounding the continuo against the constantly shifting scene. Long before the sun rises, they set out in their boats to retrieve their nets and lines. Their holds full, they return to open their market, spreading their catch on marble slabs all along the quay and the waterfront. And after they have sold everything, they will stay for long hours beside their boats, blending completely into the scenery, laying out their nets to dry, baiting their hooks, swapping stories while sipping ouzo in the sun and preparing for their next sortie out to sea.

The little shipyards where the fishing boats are repaired lend a graceful note to the island atmosphere, surrounded by brightly painted hulls drawn up on the sand.

The port is also the centre of the island's sophisticated social life. It is here that the first hotels were built when Mykonos made its tentative start as a summer resort. The roads in front of and around the port are lined by all kinds of restaurants, cafes, picturesque tavernas, traditional ouzeris and modern bars, that pulse with activity round the clock. This is where the locals take their habitual evening stroll, making the port a meeting spot for all the inhabitants in keeping with an age-old custom unaltered by time and foreign trends.

This is also where most of the island's business takes place. All day a seemingly inexhaustible stream of people passes in and out of its countless shops, which rarely close. The shops are flanked by banks, travel agencies, the Town Hall and Public Library, the Tourist Police station and airline office. In short, anything the visitor or resident could possibly wish can be found within this quarter.

The area round the port does not lack for monuments and museums either. It boasts the archaeological museum, the folk art museum, the mediaeval castle,

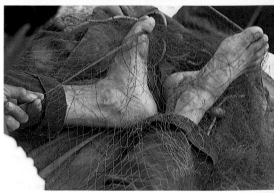

the famous church of Paraportiani, the captivating neighbourhood of Little Venice and the renowned windmills.

In about the middle of the port there is a little beach called Perris for moments of carefree relaxation.

Opposite the Town Hall, at the tip of the quay, stands the little chapel of Agios Nikolaos tis Kadenas (St. Nicholas of the Chain).

The original building was restored for the first time in 1772 by the Russian consul in Mykonos, Ioannis Voinovik. In 1912, it was renovated again, acquiring its present picturesque form and blue dome. The locals, to distinguish it from the larger church of St. Nicholas in town, also call it Ai Nikolaki tou Yialou (on the shore).

Finally, no discussion of the port of Mykonos would be complete without mentioning its trademark — its famous pair of pelicans.

The Mykoniots named them Petros and Irini, and they lived in the port for almost thirty years, eventually becoming totally tame.

They used to spend their days hovering near the restaurants and the fishermen's stands, posing for post cards or snapshots with the tourists.

It is not hard to see why Mykonos, although it belongs to the Cyclades and possesses all the features common to the other islands, stands apart from them all, thanks to small differences and idiosyncrasies. Some of these are the view of the port, the impressive houses of Alevkandra rising out of the waves, the stately windmills round town — things that from the first leave an indelible imprint on the soul and mind of anyone who comes here.

► The harbour with some cruiseships at anchor, as seen from above.
► The quay is carpeted by the fishermen's nets spread out to dry.
► The waterfront pulsates with activity round the clock.

26

Architecture in the Hora

Nevertheless, one may rightly ask what is it that makes Mykonos so picturesque and so original? What makes it stand out from all the other towns in the Cyclades and which has made it famous? An unusual, individual town plan — or better, the lack of any such plan — and an architectural style created by the practical and artistic resources of the Mykoniots, who put to such good use all the local materials and adapted them to the island's special weather conditions — strong winds, lots of sunshine — are what have made Mykonos unique.

During the Middle Ages, the whole town was confined to the castle, but even that has no similarity to the fortified citadels found in the rest of the Cyclades. While most castles in the Aegean are surrounded by strong walls and fortifications and constructed in naturally safe spots, the Kastro in Mykonos is much less prepossessing and could have offered its occupants but little protection. In essence, it consists of nothing more than the closely knit exterior walls of the houses, along with small sections of circuit wall that filled

any gaps between them. The interior of the castle contained rudimentary installations for the defence of the occupants and their survival in case of enemy attack. Over time, the present town grew up around the original mediaeval settlement, its greatest expansion taking place after the second world war.

Many people have compared the Hora to a honeycomb. And, in fact, one's first impression on seeing it today is of a complicated yet uniform entity of houses, inextricably united and interconnected by a labyrinthine network of miniscule streets. An infinite number of narrow lanes, all paved with flagstones and decorated with paint and flowers, penetrate everywhere.

The houses, so close they often touch each other, have the same external proportions. They all have two-storeys — in earlier days, the ground floor was used as a storeroom — with two openings, a door and a window, on each floor. Access to the first floor is always by a straight flight of steps that ends in a balcony, while the door to the ground floor opens directly onto the street. The

feature which differentiates each house and gives the characteristic note to the whole town is the touches of colour in the banisters and balcony railings, the painted gates and the bright shutters and doors.

The combination of good taste and practicality in the vernacular architecture of Mykonos gives it elements of unparalleled plasticity, such as its "katastegia" and dovecotes. To economize on space, rooms would even be built out over the street, bridging the gap between houses. Unfortunately, very few of these "katastegia" exist today. What has been preserved are the graceful arches above the alleyways that used to support them.

Doves and pigeons were prized from very early on in the Cyclades both as a source of food and of exceptional fertiliser. In Mykonos, however, the construction of the dovecote evolved into a real jewel, adorning the island house with original and artistic patterns. The chimneys, known on the island as "kapasi", with their varied shapes and decoration, the built-in ledges on the flat roofs, and even the cylindrical, white-washed water conduits create a composition distinguished for its plasticity, splendid aesthetics and individuality within homogeneity. In speaking of Mykonos, the architect Ar. Romanos stated the view that the town, with its white-washed streets, painted staircases and flowerpots, gives the impression of a "familiar and protective place", where nevertheless the sun, the wind, the blue sky and the sight of the sea bring one back to reality.

To these elements two more should be added which are typical of the island. The first is related to the unusual shape of the Hora's picturesque lanes and

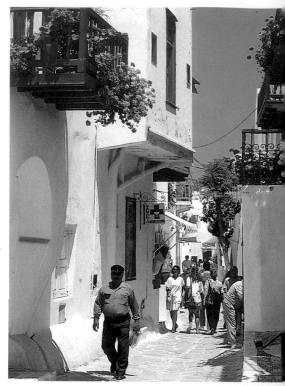

The winding lanes, the dovecotes, the staircases - everything in Mykonos has its own personality.

alleys. Due to restrictions on space, the Mykoniots are unable to build houses with gardens or even courtyards. They do have the right, however, to a small piece of the street that passes in front of their home. In order to proclaim their ownership, they have acquired the custom of painting the stone slabs that "belong" to them a different colour from the rest of the lane and the adjacent houses, creating thus marvellous contrasts with the dazzling white walls. The second element refers to one of the "means" of transport. Because most of the alleyways in the Hora are too narrow to accommodate cars, the inhabitants make frequent use of donkeys!

It is really touching to see the care they give to those endearing beasts of burden and the way in which they decorate them at every opportunity. Furthermore, donkeys are also the preferred mode of selling local farm produce. Every morning, the country people come in from the farms lying outside town with their donkeys laden with heavy baskets and hawk their goods loudly in the streets. This is a display of island life that has remained unaffected by progress and which has become a tradition.

Tiny chapels pop up amongst the houses, people meet in the narrow alleys, patiently embroidered curtains hang in the windows and wooden balconies jut over the streets.

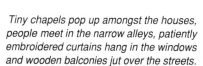

The Paraportiani Church

But what are the absolute "musts" for a visitor to Mykonos's Hora to see?

First on the list has to be that rare example of vernacular ecclesiastical architecture: the Paraportiani church. It is built on the edge of the Kastro district, and as you approach it, you see only its facade silhouetted stark white against the deep blue of the sea and the sky. The name "Paraportiani" derives from its setting, having been constructed between the sea and the small gate ("paraporti") of the castle. In reality, it is not one church but a compact complex of five chapels, erected over the centuries on two distinct levels. The date of the first church is lost in the mist of tradition, and even today unfortunately scientific opinion cannot concur on when it was built.

Agii Anargyri is considered to be the oldest of the chapels. It is said to date to the late 14th or early 15th century, being completed in its final form in the 17th century. The other four chapels were subsequently added to it. They are arranged in the shape of the letter "T", with Agii Anargyri at the centre of the horizontal "arm", the chapel of Agios Efstathios to the east, Agios Sozon to the west, and Agia Anastasia below in the middle of the vertical "leg". The main church, dedicated to the Virgin, was added considerably later in the western part of the complex above that of Agios Efstathios.

The interior of the churches is plain, but what little decoration does exist is impressive, consisting of old icons protraying the saints. This spare appearance, coupled with the dim lighting that contrasts so completely with the brilliant white of the exterior, instills awe and a feeling of religiosity in the visitor.

Externally, the five churches appear as one united whole — a composition of successive white cubic forms, inextricably joined to one another.

The passage of time has played an important role in forging the way the Paraportiani looks today. Ravages caused by the weather and other natural factors at various points have yet to be

repaired. They are simply covered by whitewash, applied at regular intervals. This unwitting contribution to time's wear and tear led Vasilios Kyriazopoulos to describe it as "being simultaneously engendered by both time and man". In the memories of the Mykonians, the Paraportiani is strongly linked with all the trials and tribulations that their island and their homes have suffered. The first church was built at virtually the same time as the castle and within its precincts, during the arduous Middle Ages.

This was a period fraught with pirates and pillaging and successive occupations by the powerful states of Europe, which continually oppressed the few residents of the little town. The church of Agii Anargyri was something that gave comfort and strength to the faithful.

When later external threats to the island diminished, the Mykonians were still exposed to daily danger.
Their lives were bound to the sea, the main source of work and wealth for the island. Harsh weather conditions posed and still pose a permanent hazard to the sailor. In all these difficult moments, the Virgin Paraportiani remains a place of comfort and consolation for all.
The religious sentiments of the

The Paraportiani:
five chuches moulded into one unique,
brilliant white complex of remarkable
shapes and planes.

Mykonians, like those of most islanders, are very intense.
Thus, they never fail to make use of the numerous opportunities offered by the Orthodox Church to honour the Virgin, the protectress of the island.

At all her feast days (in August and November, etc.), the Paraportiani is festooned with decorations by the congregation, filled with pilgrims, and the focus of interest for large crowds of people, both locals and not.

The location of this monument, next to the sea and the castle; its complex external form, which distinguishes it from all the other buildings in the Hora; its venerable age — all have made it into a symbolic place, where the human and the divine, history and tradition, reality and myth, the contemporary and the legendary, the past and the present meet on a daily basis.

The churches in the Hora vie among themselves for beauty and originality.

Little Venice

In the chapter on the Hora of Mykonos and its original architecture, we described a picture that more or less applies to all the neighbourhoods in the town. One of these, however, stands apart, having been built in its own separate style and having had its own distinct history. This is Alevkandra, the much beloved artists' quarter. Standing virtually amidst the waves, it has rightly won the epithet, "the Venice of Mykonos". Its other name, Alevkandra, was given it by the Mykonians in the old days, for it was there that they went to wash or "levkanoun" their clothes.

The houses in Little Venice started being built around the mid 18th century by rich merchants and sea captains. Their construction coincided with the development of shipping and trade and the emergence of the first bourgeois classes. The "karavokyraiika" (boat-like) houses are unlike the rest of the buildings in the Hora. Most of them have three storeys and spacious interiors. Their facades, though they possess many of the traditional Mykonian architectural elements described earlier, also display many neoclassical features

and have many more windows. On the side of the house that is washed by the waves, a small door permits direct access to the sea! On this side, too, there is invariably a small wooden closed-in balcony, next to the traditional open one.

Why did the rich sea captains of Mykonos choose this specific spot and this type of architecture for their mansions? One explanation has been put forward.

Historians write that, in the old days, beginning about the 16th century, Mykonos was a pirate haven. According to G.B. Leon, many island Greeks turned to piracy, either independently or in collusion with the Barbary corsairs. A. Romanos states it as fact that up to the end of the 17th century, the Greek pirates robbed and pillaged along the coast, based on islands which could afford some concealment. It appears from many accounts that Mykonos was such an island. Piracy in fact made the islanders wealthy and helped to create a small core of bourgeoisie, the first urban class. The houses of the rich sea captains in Little Venice — in direct

contact with the sea, their little sea-
doors leading directly or through
courtyards to underground storerooms
— were used for the secret transfer and
caching of pirate loot.

The houses of Little Venice, each with
its own history, linked with the legends
and names of centuries gone by, exude
an atmosphere of romance and mystery,
while captivating us with their beauty
and charm. This neighbourhood has
become the favourite of artists seeking
inspiration in its thrilling traditions. Thus
Little Venice is, along with the
Paraportiani, the most written about and
most painted part of the island.

The attraction exerted by Alevkandra on
both artists and casual visitors cannot be
attributed to just one of its

*Houses that seem to grow out of the sea, octopus
drying in the sun, little tables set alongside the waves
for a view of the sunset - a few of the features that
make Alevkandra so extraordinary.*

idiosyncrasies.

Many elements are woven together here to produce a unique neighbourhood that can be described unequivocally as having "personality". From the architectural point of view, one remains in admiration of the perfect harmonization of the Mykonos balcony with the neoclassical iron work or the stark Cycladic facade with the more elaborate neoclassical decoration above the main entrance to the house. As regards the setting, the close proximity of the water and the unrestricted view of the sea, so intertwined with stories of pirates, awaken our imagination and transport us to those long ago times, around the end of the Middle Ages, making us feel that even today anything could happen from one moment to the next. The steep alleyways, narrow and evocative, add to this conviction. The history of this quarter and of the people who lived here, the rich blend of myth and tradition, have endowed Alevkandra with a fascination that transfixes us and which cannot be found anywhere else in the Cyclades.

The boat looks about to enter the house and the houses seem about to set sail.

Windmills and Traditions

On Mykonos the wind blows without cease for 200 to 300 days each year. The wind is a blessing, offering relief from the fiery heatof the sun.
Whoever sets foot on Mykonos has to surrender tothese two elements.
This is why the largest tree is a thyme bush, why all the houses have closed courtyards and high walls ... for some protection against the wind. Both man and nature have adapted to the weather conditions, and everything here has been styled to serve human needs.
If the walls are coated once or twice each year with whitewash, this is to reflect the sweltering heat. If there are mills, it is because the wind was harnessed to grind wheat and barley. And if the women wear kerchiefs on their heads, it is to keep the wind from ruffling their hair.
Nothing on the island is a result of happenstance or oversight, but developed as a direct consequence of the needs of the inhabitants.
As to the power of the winds on Mykonos, tradition maintains that whenever an unmarried stranger sets

foot on the island and drinks water from the "Three Springs", he will marry a girl from Mykonos. He will be so unaccustomed to the force of the wind that he will lose his mind and will to resist. With reason, then, the windmill is the symbol of Mykonos, though it is found throughout the Cyclades.
The mill is a circular structure with wooden conelike roof.
In earlier times there must have been about 15 mills on the island. The higher ones ground the island's wheat, the lower ones, ten in number, the wheat that came from other places. The millers were paid in kind. The end product, the flour, was either reloaded onto boats or made into bread and rusks in the ovens in the Hora.
These supplied the ships that stopped at Mykonos for precisely this purpose.
Flour grinding and bread baking, combined with shipping and the wool and cotton crafts, brought economic growth to Mykonos in the early 19th century.
The Mykonians' exploitation of their strategic position on the trade routes

A concerto in white; white houses, white windmills.

and their natural resources, including the wind, made the island one of the main revictualling stations in the Aegean. Later, in the 20th century, other natural resources — the sun and the sea — along with their architecture and proximity to Delos helped it to become a popular resort.

The wind that blows most of the year used to grind the island's grain. In the past there must have been about fifteen windmills.

*S*ightseeing

A guided tour of the Hora of Mykonos begins with the Kastro district near the port. Here the **Town Hall** stands out, its sloping red tile roof distinguishing it from the rest of the buildings. Erected in the 18th century, it was constructed on the initiative of the Russian consul on the island, Ioannis Voinovik, during the brief Russian domination of the Cyclades (1770-1774).

The **Archaeological Museum**, a neoclassical building of 1901, lies near the Town Hall. Most of its exhibits — except for the vase depicting the Trojan Horse, which was found only recently on Mykonos — come from the neighbouring island of Rheneia. In ancient times, Rheneia was designated a necropolis after death and burial were forbidden on Delos. As a consequence, the museum contains a large number of grave ornaments and stelae, as well as various types of pottery and jewelry from the Early Geometric down to the Hellenistic and Roman eras.

Before leaving the Kastro area, one should also visit the **Folk Art Museum**, founded and endowed by professor Vassilis Kyriazopoulos, a native of Mykonos. It is a fact that Mykonos, in comparison with neighbouring islands, has little archaeological interest and an insignificant ancient history. Nevertheless, these deficiencies are more than compensated for by the wealth of its folk tradition, which has its roots in the late Middle Ages. Professor Kyriazopoulos made it his goal, starting in 1962, to collect all the arts and crafts, national and historic memorabilia of the island in a lovely turn-of-the-century building. Thanks to the constant and persistent efforts of its founder, the Folk Art Museum has enriched its collections with numerous objects of daily use, furniture, naive Byzantine sculptures, objects taken from Revolutionary ships, old costumes from the area, and a great deal more. It thus recreates for the visitor the daily life of another era, when conditions were perhaps harsher but the people surely

► Grave stele from the Rheneia necropolis. Archaeological Museum of Mykonos.

more genuine.

In the adjoining quarter, Matoyanni, a 19th century mansion that once belonged to Admiral Nikolaos Sourmelis, houses the **Maritime Museum of the Aegean**. This museum, too, owes its existence to the deep love of the Mykonians for their special homeland: it was founded with a grant from the Mykonian shipowner, Drakopoulos. The architecture of the building itself merits the attention of the visitor. This

traditional Mykonian house has been restored with great care and is surrounded by a large, lush and well-tended garden, a real oasis in the Hora. Although the museum has only been open since 1985, it contains a fine collection of ship models from the Minoan era to the last century, as well as a valuable collection of coins depicting naval scenes.

Next to the Maritime Museum is another building donated by Drakopoulos,

dedicated to folklore. This is the famous **Lena's House**, it too a representative example of 19th century architecture, which has been arranged and furnished in the style prevailing then. Also situated in the vicinity are the **Three Wells** (Tria Pigadia) that until recently used to supply the Hora with water.

Matoyannis is also the home of the **Municipal Art Gallery**, in which works by Greek and foreign artists are exhibited. A bit outside town, to the

◄ *Bronze statuette of a Kouros, which formed the handle of a utensil. It was found on Rheneia, in the pit where the Athenians in 426/425 B.C. cast the bones of the dead whish had been transferred to the island from Delos. Archaeological Museum of Mykonos.*

▲ *Cycladic vase decorated with female figures and swans, 7th c. B.C. Found in the Hora, Mykonos. Archaeological Museum of Mykonos.*

► *Detail of a depicting the Trojan Horse on an amphora from Tinos, 7th c. B.C. Found in the Hora, Mykonos. Archaeological Museum of Mykonos.*

south, a branch of the Athens School of Fine Arts was opened not long ago, both recognizing and augmenting the importance of the Mykonos landscape as a source of artistic inspiration. The school is set in the midst of an idyllic estate and is open to both Greeks and foreigners.

The **Municipal Library** lies in the centre of the Hora. A gift of the Mykonian historian, I. Meletopoulos, it contains several rare books and manuscripts. The building housing it dates to the early 18th century and belonged to the noted Mavrogenis family, which played a major role in the island's history.

Among the countless other sights in Mykonos, two shops are worthy of special mention. They belong to personalities who have won international acclaim in the world of haute couture and they have both chosen Mykonos as their permanent residence and place of inspiration. One of them is Yannis Galatis, the famous Mykonian fashion designer, who for years has showing his fabulous creations in Manto Mavrogeni square; the other is the self-taught Sophia Thanopoulou, who displays her own fabrics and jewelry in the Maroulina boutique.

Of particular interest are the numerous churches, big and small, scattered about the town and countryside. In Alevkandra, for example, there is the **Catholic church**, erected in the 16th century, repaired in the 17th and again in the 18th, when it was enriched by several paintings from Venice. In recent years it is only open from April to October. Next to it is the Orthodox Cathedral, the **Virgin Mother of God** or **Pigadiotissa**, the richest of Mykonos's churches with lovely icons and a beautiful interior.

Attic red figured vases. Archaeological Museum of Mykonos.

Another interesting church is **Agia Eleni** (St. Helen) of the Kastro. It is one of the largest on the island and contains some old Byzantine icons. It was the cathedral until 1878.

What is truly remarkable on Mykonos is the incredible number of tiny churches that pop up unexpectedly in every corner of town.

They owe their existence to both the deep religious beliefs of the inhabitants and the many sailors who in time of danger vowed to build a church if they survived. This also accounts for the fact that so many of them are dedicated to St. Nicholas, the patron saint of seafarers. The presence of a picturesque church, simple and unadorned, at every turn is one of the most attractive aspects of the Hora.

The Rest of the Island

Having said so much about the Hora, we must not forget the Mykonos countryside, which is equally interesting, dotted as it is with extended farmhouses and picturesque chapels and rimmed with fantastic beaches. The hills and valleys of Mykonos, being especially bereft of trees and other vegetation, are dun-coloured and greyish like the earth and rocks, except for splashes of dazzling white, bright blue and green from the farmhouses, church domes, doors, shutters and cactuslike plants.

Until a few decades ago, when you said "horia" or villages in Mykonos, you were referring to the landed wealth of the peasants — the farmhouses and outbuildings (barns, ovens, etc.) circumscribed by exquisite dry stone walls. These farms were virtually self-sufficient.

The most striking feature of the countryside, however, is the extraordinary number of churches that one encounters all over the place. Most of them are incorporated into the farm buildings and further strength their autonomy, acting as private charnel houses. They are there because the Mykonians uphold the tradition that forbids removing the dead from the place where they lived. The rest of the dispersed chapels are mainly the outcome of sailors' vows during moments of peril.

Whatever else it may be, the Mykonos "horio" is the genuine vernacular architectural creation of people who managed to eke out a life from the barren land, their only resources the wind, the sun, the sea and the ingenuity that comes with poverty.

Setting out from the Hora for the north of the island, the road cuts through the rocky scenery of Mykonos to arrive at the village of **Tourlos** on the bay of the same name. This bay, now the anchorage for cruiseships, is the safest harbour on the island from the north wind. It is lined with beautiful beaches, comfortable hotels and boasts the two lovely churches of **St. George** and **St. George of the Cave** (Agios Georgios tou Spilianou).

Continuing northward, not far from Tourlos, one comes to the bay of **Agios**

The sun and the sea are the riches of Mykonos.

Stefanos, which takes its name from the little church nearby. This area has undergone enormous development for tourism in recent years.

From Agios Stefanos, a good dirt road runs parallel to the pretty beach of Houlaika, passing the chapel of **Agios Sostis** to end at **Cape Armenistis**. Here the landscape is completely different; gone are the tranquil beaches, here the coast is wild and awesome, with huge rocks plunging abruptly into the sea. A

cluster of these rocks support a 100 metre tall lighthouse, built in 1889 to light the strait between Mykonos and Tinos.

In the northeast, the road forks, one leg passing by **Marath**i and the 17th century monastery of **Agios Panteleimon** to arrive at the beaches of **Panormos** and **Agios Sostis**, the other leading to the beach of **Ftelia,** which has become a well-known centre for windsurfing. The natural layout of this beach and the

constant winds make for ideal conditions for this sport.

Between Ftelia and Panormos lies the **Black Cave** (Mavri Spilia), accessible from either beach.

Not too long ago, many tools and objects from the Neolithic era were discovered in the cave.

The village of **Ano Mera** is the first stop on the road to the east coast; it lies virtually in the centre of the island and is the largest settlement after the Hora.

It's hard to say which of Mykonos's beaches is your favourite.

1. Paradise

2. Super Paradise

3. Elia

4. Ornos

1	4
2 3	

► *Psarou*

From here one can visit the hill of **Palaiokastro**, where the ruined castle of the Ghisi rulers presides over the bay of Panormos and the 18th century monastery of Palaiokastro. Some scholars maintain that this was also the site of the ancient capital of Mykonos, based on finds from excavations on the hill.

A bit further south is the **Monastery** of the **Virgin Tourliani**, the patroness of the island. This is one of the most important buildings on Mykonos. Erected in the 16th century, expanded and repaired in the 18th and 19th, it possesses valuable icons, a marvellous iconostasis and a marble belltower. Below this monastery is yet another, the monastery of **Agios Georgios Ambelokipon** (St. George of the Vineyards), dating to the 17th century. The road ends at the beaches of **Kalafatis** in the north and of **Agia Anna, Kalo Livadi** and **Elia** in the south.

At the small peninsula of **Dimastos,** which separates the bay of Kalafatis from Kalo Livadi, there appears to have been another prehistoric settlement. The east coast with all its sights and lovely beaches is very popular with tourists today.

But the most developed and famous resort area on Mykonos continues to be the southern part of the island.

This is where its internationally renowned beaches, **Paradise** and **Super Paradise**, attract hordes of Greek and foreign nature worshippers each summer. Accessible by caique from Platys Yialos or by bad road from the Hora, they are lined with nightclubs, restaurants and fully equipped camp sites. The road goes first to **Psarou** and **Platys Yialos**, resorts with seaside tavernas, comfortable hotels and sophisticated nightlife.

The area is also not without archaeological interest.

A bit further east at Linos and Portes are

the ruins of two towers from the classical era and an ancient well with steps leading into it, known as the well of **Yiannaros.**

Finally, the peninsula of **Diakoftis**, south of the Hora, has witnessed much development in recent years. Bordered by the coves of **Korfos** and **Ornos,** this is where the most luxurious hotel complexes are situated.

On the coast west of the Hora, directly opposite Delos, is the fashionable beach of **Ai Yiannis**, an ideal place to watch the fantastic sunsets over the sacred island.

All the island's beaches have golden sand and calm, crystalline waters.

1. Psarou

3. Pisso Livadi

4. Platys Yialos

5. Agios Stefanos

6. Kalafatis

1	3	
2	4	5

Delos

The sacred island of Delos lies just 1 nautical mile south of the western tip of Mykonos.

It has an oblong shape, an area of 3.43 square kilometres, and a rocky coastline. Its terrain, composed mostly of granite and gneiss, is barren and rough. It is generally flat, except for Kynthos hill at an altitude of 112 metres.

The valley of a dry river, the Inopus, cuts through the island from north to south. In ancient times, this sacred river was thought to have its source in the Nile. It flowed into the bay of Skardanas.

In even earlier times, Delos was called Ortygia, or Quail island.

Mythology relates that its present name derives from the word "A- delos" (invisible), a reference to the time when it floated around the Aegean attached to no fixed spot. After the birth there of Apollo, it became anchored and visible or "delos".

Its geographic location, in a key place in the centre of the Aegean, led to its becoming an important way station for ships sailing between the Greek mainland, the islands and the coast of Asia Minor. As both a sacred place and a major harbour, it put its stamp on the space around it, the Cyclades according to one theory taking their name from the circle or "kyklos" they form around Delos.

MYTHOLOGY

Delos, uninhabited today, was one of the most revered religious centres of the Greek world. Legend connected it with the birth of Apollo, god of light and prophesy.

Homer in his "Hymn to Apollos" recounts how Leto, in desperation, searched high and low for a place that would allow her to give birth to the fruit of her union with Zeus. Everywhere she turned, her plea was rejected, because no spirit dared risk the wrath of Hera. When, finally, she set foot on Delos, she addressed herself to the island, saying: "So poor is your earth", what man could ever be induced to set foot here? Neither cow nor sheep can graze here; neither grapevines nor any form of tree will ever prosper on you, such is the dryness that scourges you. But if my son should be born here, then you could nurture your people, because the beasts that men would bring here to be sacrificed would be beyond counting." Leto swore on the holy waters of the Styx that the god about to be born would

never forget the barren island and that he
would found his foremost sanctuary here.
In another variation on the myth, the lyric
poet Pindar mentions that Delos was an
island that floated in the Aegean,
travelling here and there with no fixed
location. The mortals called it Ortygia,
the gods Asteria, because from afar it
shone like a star. As soon as Leto set
foot on Ortygia or Asteria, four columns
rose out of the deep, fixing the island
firmly in place so that it never moved
again.
Callimachus, the Alexandrian poet, in his
verses on the sacred isle, maintains that
Delos was a nymph on whom Zeus
turned his attentions. She, however, out
of respect for Hera, preferred to become
a star and fall into the sea than accept
his advances. And thus Asteria was
created. To punish her Zeus made her
soil barren and parched and kept her
wandering in the sea. Leto, in her own
wanderings, saw her and begged her to
take her in. The island tenderly agreed.
As soon as Apollo came into the world, to
reward her for her hospitality, columns
rose up to support her from the deep.
From that moment on, she took the name
Delos; for the first time, her position
became manifest.

HISTORY: MILESTONES IN THE LIFE
OF THE ISLAND
Delos began to be inhabited around
2800 B.C., as evidenced by the ruins of a
prehistoric settlement excavated on Mt.
Kynthos.
These first inhabitants may have been
the Lelegians or, as Thucydides
maintains, unverifiably however, the
Carians.
Round about 1050-950 B.C., the Ionians
arrived on the island, bringing with them
the worship of their protector, Apollo.
By the 8th century B.C., Delos was
developing trade with the Eastern
Mediterranean (Armenia, Syria). It was
the headquarters of the amphictiony of
the Ionian cities. During the same era,
especially brilliant festivals in honour of
Apollo, the Delia, were being held every

year, drawing Ionians from all over the Greek world. They included athletic, dance and song contests, and provided a marvellous opportunity for those assembled to do business. In this way, Delos quickly evolved into a centre not only for religion but also for trade.

An important factor in attracting merchants to the island was that, being sacred, Delos was under the protection of Zeus and its privileged status was inviolable. Those who increasingly visited it were guaranteed safety and ran no risk of being looted.

The island's illustriousness in the Archaic years (800-500 B.C.) was so great that its influence spread to the realm of politics.

In the middle of the 7th century B.C., itappears to have fallen under the sway of Naxos. By the second half of the 6th century B.C., the Athenians had their eye on it. In 540 B.C., Peisistratus, the tyrant of Athens, ordered the sanctuary purified and the burial ground removed from the city. The tombs were moved to an area where they could not be seen from the sacred precinct.

With the end of the Persian Wars, Delos found itself once again under the hegemony of the Athenians.

In 478 B.C. the First Athenian Confederacy was founded with headquarters in Delos. It convened in the temple of Apollo, which also held the Treasury with the contributions of the allied city-states. In 454 B.C. with the Athenians assuming greater power, the Confederacy Treasury was transferred to Athens and kept on the Acropolis on the pretext that it would be safer there. At this time, the Athenians were responsible

for both the formalities surrounding the worship of the god and for the administration of the Sanctuary's finances; they do not appear to have exerted any influence over the island's other affairs.

In the winter of 426-425 B.C., the Athenians were threatened by plague. In an attempt to propitiate the god, they declared the whole island of Delos sacred and imposed a second purification on it. They dug up all the

◄ The Terrace of the Lions. What remains of the row of lions which had been erected by the Naxians in the late 7th c. B.C. The lions, seated on their haunches, face east in the direction of the Sacred Lake.

► The cistern of the Theatre. Divided into nine compartments, it collected water from the Orchestra, which was used to supply the town.

► Detail of a mosaic floor.

graves and took the remains and funerary objects to Rheneia, where they were buried in an enormous ditch. From then on birth and death were forbidden to take place on Delos; anyone about to give birth or die was removed to Rheneia.

That same year the Athenians ruled that the Delia would be held every five years. With the end of the Peloponnesian War in 404 B.C. and the defeat of the Athenians, Delos regained its autonomy.

But not for long; only ten years later it was once again under the domination of Athens, and it remained so until the Macedonian kings gained supremacy over the Greek city-states in 315-314 B.C. Then Delos became the religious centre of the League of Islanders, which was

► *Detail of a mosaic floor from the House of the Dolphins. The corners of the floor are decorated with figures of Eros riding dolphins.*

▼ *The House of Cleopatra. The statues of this lady and her husband, Dioskouridis.*

subject to the Ptolemies of Egypt.
The Alliance dissolved in 250 B.C. when
Delos fell under the custody of the
Macedonians. This period represents a
milestone in the history of the island
because it marked the start of the
transformation of the holy city into a
major trade centre. From that time until
about 100 B.C., Delos enjoyed great
prosperity.
Its population increased, its complexion
changed. The worship of other gods was
introduced.

With the defeat of the Macedonian king,
Perseas, by the Romans, Delos and its
sanctuary were conceded to the
Athenians by decision of the Senate in
166 B.C.; the port, however, was
declared to be free. The whole
population of Delos was dispatched into
exile and replaced by Athenian colonists.
With the destruction of the important
ports of Carchedon and Corinth by the
Romans in 146 B.C., Delos became the
centre for trade in the Aegean. This
resulted once again in the diversification

*of its inhabitants with the influx of
merchants from Italy and the Levant. The
city acquired a cosmopolitan character.
Between 100 and 90 B.C., Delos under
the mantle of Rome reached the peak of
its prosperity.
The first blow fell in 88 B.C. when
Mithridates, king of the Pontus, wishing
to injure the Romans, invaded and
ransacked Delos. Thousands of
inhabitants were killed, among them
numerous Romans, and the island was
denuded of its wealth.*

*The second catastrophe occurred in 69
B.C. Mithridates' ally, Athenodorus and
his pirate cohorts, destroyed the city and
a great many of the residents were taken
into slavery.
The construction of new ports in Italy and
the Levant resulted in the decline and
eventual obscurity of the once eminent
Delos. In later centuries it was of no
importance. And so it remained,*

"invisible" and forgotten until 1872-1873, when the French School of Archaeology began its systematic excavations which are still under way today.

THE ARCHAEOLOGICAL SITE
Delos is one vast archaeological site. Access to the island today is from the ancient harbour, on the northwest coast. Starting from the harbour, the main ruins one encounters are:

In **the area of the Sanctuary**
The Agora of the Competialists or Hermaists erected in the 2nd century B.C. This was the centre of the merchants from Italy. The Competialists were Italian slaves and free men who worshiped the divinities who watched over the crossroads. The ancient avenue, the Sacred Way, which initially leads eastward and then to the north, is lined by several buildings. First on the left is the **Stoa of Philip**, built in 210 B.C. by Philip V of Macedonia as an offering to Apollo. On the right side of the road is the **South Stoa**, a 3rd century B.C. building paid for by the kings of Pergamon. East of the South Stoa is the **Agora of the Delians**, also known as the the Square Stoa. Southeast of the Agora are the ruins of a 5th century Christian basilica dedicated to Agios Kirykos (St. Quiricus).
The Sanctuary of Apollo lies to the northeast of the Stoa of Philip.

The Sanctuary of Apollo
The main entrance to the Sanctuary, the **Propylaia,** is to the south. It is still standing in the form given it in the 2nd century B.C. To its right is the **Oikos of the Naxians** (late 7th/early 6th century B.C.), an offering by the people of Naxos to Apollo.
On the north wall of the Oikos one can still see the base of the colossal statue of Apollo that once stood there. Measuring about 7 metres tall, it too was a gift of the Naxians. The **Sacred Way** passed in

The House of Dionysos, in the Theatre Quarter.

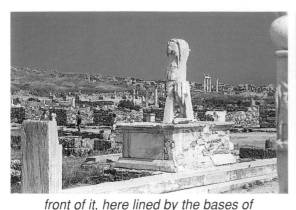

front of it, here lined by the bases of various votive offerings. To the west of the Oikos is the **Stoa of the Naxians** (mid 6th century B.C.)
Northeast of the Stoa is the **Keraton** or **Keratinos Altar**, an almost square building. It may have housed an old altar made of horns and antlers ("kerata"), around which there was a frieze representing the adventures of Theseus in Crete and dancing the dance of the cranes upon his return to Athens after killing the Minotaur. It was erected by the Athenians in the mid 4th century B.C.
Southeast of the Stoa of Philip and east of the Oikos of the Naxians are three important **Temples** to **Apollo,** one next to the other. The oldest is the "Porinos Naos", constructed with limestone ("porolithos") in the third quarter of the 6th century B.C. by the Athenians.
The middle temple, Doric in style, was also erected by the Athenians but in Pentelic marble in 425 B.C. The southernmost and largest of the temples is known as the "Temple of the Delians". Construction was begun by the Athenians in 478 B.C. and was completed by the Delians at the end of the 4th century. It is the only temple on the island with a colonnade on all sides and it dominates the sanctuary.
The three temples are flanked on the north by five buildings in the form of small temples, the **Treasuries**, which contained the portable offerings of the city-states to the god. It is possible that some of them may also have been used

as inns where the pilgrims could sleep or eat. To the east of the Treasuries is the **Prytaneion**, a 5th century B.C. building where the overseers of the Sanctuary met. To the east of it is an unusual oblong building (4th/3rd century B.C.) called, mistakenly the **Monument to the Bulls**. It was built to commemorate a naval victory but earned its name from the decoration on its frieze.
The north side of the Sanctuary of Apollo is closed off by the **Stoa of Antigonos**, built in the 3rd century B.C. by the Macedonian king, Antigonos Gonatas.
To the northwest of the Sanctuary are the granite foundations of the **Artemesion or Temple of Artemis**, Apollo's sister. It was erected in the 2nd century B.C. upon the ruins of a 7th century temple.
Near the outer side of the Stoa of Antigonos is the **Minoe Fountain**, a rectangular cistern, dating to the late 6th or early 5th century B.C.
In the vicinity of the Sacred Lake
To the north of the Sanctuary of Apollo lies the **Agora of the Italians**, where the Italian colonists used to gather. It is the largest monument on the island. Near it is the **Dodekatheon,** a small temple

▲ One of the square pillars from the Sanctuary of Dionysos.

▲ The Terrace of the Lions.

➤ Detail of the mosaic floor from the House of the Trident.

➤ pp. 88-89
Detail of a mosaic floor in which Dionysos is depicted on the back of a panther wreathed in vines.

dedicated to the twelve gods of Olympos and the **Letoon,** dedicated to the mother of Apollo and Artemis, Leto. A 6th century B.C. building, it is unusual in that its orientation is towards the Sanctuary of Apollo.

The avenue passing to the north of the Letoon leads into the **Terrace of the Lions**, built by the Naxians in the 7th century B.C. Originally, nine or more lions stood here; only five have survived to the present.

Southwest of the Lion Terrace is the **Institution of the Poseidoniasts** of Berytos, a centre for the merchants from Beirut who worshipped Poseidon, and to the southeast are two **Palaistras** (Wrestling Gyms), the **Lake Palaistra** and the **Granite Paliastra.**

The **Sacred Lake** lies to the west of the Lion Terrace. Dry since 1926, this is the lake mentioned by Herodotus as the "Hoop Lake", so-called because of its shape.

The north precinct

North of the Sanctuary is the north precinct of the ancient city, whose most important buildings are the houses of Diadoumenos, the Lake, the Comedians and Cleopatra. Some of them contain marvellous mosaics.

The Theatre Quarter

South of the Sanctuary the Theatre Quarter also has several houses decorated with lovely mosaic floors, such as those of the Dolphins, the Masks, the Tridents and Dionysos.

Northwest of the house of the Masks stands the ruined **theatre**, a construction of the 2nd century B.C. able to accommodate about 5,500 spectators.

The Kynthos Quarter

East of the Theatre Quarter are the ruins of several buildings: the **Sanctuaries of the Foreign Gods**; the three **Serapions** (A, B, C.), **Egyptian sanctuaries**; the **Sanctuary of the Syrian Gods**; and the **Cabeirion** or **Samothrakion.** To the right of Serapion C is the **Heraion,** dedicated to Hera. From here the road leads to Mt. Kynthos, on whose summit can be seen

the ruined sanctuaries of **Kynthian Zeus** and **Kynthian Athena**. Traces of a prehistoric settlement have also been unearthed here.

The **Gymnasium** and the **Stadium** are in the northeast part of the island.

About 1 kilometre south of the Sacred Harbour on the bay of Phournae there are more ruins, including the **Sanctuary of Asclepios** with its Doric temple, Treasury, Propylon, Infirmary and Dining Hall.

THE DELOS MUSEUM

The Museum houses finds from Delos of the Archaic and Classical periods. Archaic sculpture is exhibited in the main hall. The north room contains mosaics, frescoes, and household utensils, while in the south room examples of pottery from prehistoric times to the 4th century B.C. are on view. Other exhibits include Hellenistic sculptures, grave steles from Rheneia, mosaics and frescoes.

◄ View of the Agora of the Competialists or Hermaists.

◄ One of the square pillars from the Sanctuary of Dionysos, which was founded about 300 B.C. An enourmous phallus, a symbol of worship of the god, was placed on the top of each pillar.

▲ Panther, detail from the mosaic floor of the House of Dionysos.

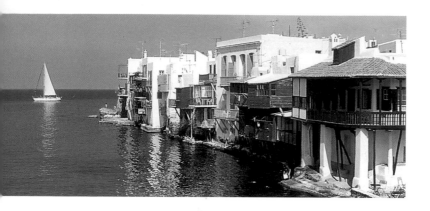

Useful information

HOW TO GET THERE

By boat

Boats leave Piraeus and Rafina (27 km. east of Athens) daily for Mykonos. The length of the trip from Piraeus is about 6 to 6 1/2 hours, from Rafina 5 1/2 to 6 hours. Piraeus can be reached by metro (central stations include Victoria, Omonia, Monastiraki) or by bus. Rafina is linked to Athens by buses departing from Mavromataion Street at the Pedion tou Areos not far from the Archaeological Museum (Tel.: 01/821.0872).

Information on boat schedules can be obtained from the Harbour Police at Piraeus (01/451.1311), the Harbour Master at Rafina (0294/22300) and at the ticket agencies in both ports.

In summer Flying Dolphins (hydrofoils) also serve some of the Cyclades islands, sailing from Rafina several times a day. Call / 0294/25100 for information. The trip takes about 2 1/2 hours. Another fast means of transport is the catamarans sailing from Flisvos on the Saronic coast (tel.: 01/4110461, 4129510-11).

Other connections

Many of the above boats also sail to the islands of Andros, Tinos, Syros and the other neighbouring Cyclades.

There are fewer regularly scheduled connections with Ikaria and Samos, as well as seasonal links with Heraklion, Skiathos and Thessaloniki.

Smaller boats also make local trips among the southern Cyclades, i.e. Paros, Naxos, the Koufonisia, Amorgos, Ios and Santorini.

Finally, there are of course daily sailings to the archaeological site at Delos.

By plane

Mykonos is linked by charter flights with various European cities. There are also several Olympic Airlines flights per day between Athens and Mykonos. For information call Olympic Airlines in Athens, 01/961.6161. Direct flights also exist between Santorini, Heraklion and Rhodes.

WHEN YOU ARRIVE

Where to stay

In hotels, pensions, guesthouses,

bungalows and furnished apartments. Many of these can be found in the Hora as well as other parts of the island, such as Agios Stefanos, Kalafatis, Ornos, Platys Yialos, Tourlosand they are distributed among five categories.

You can also stay at one of Mykonos's two campsites: at Paranga or at Paradise (Kalamopodi), 6 kilometres from the Hora. The latter is open from April to late October (tel.: 0289/22129, 22025).

Villas and rooms are available for rent. For more information about accommodation, get in touch with the Hotel Chamber of Greece by writing to their office at 24 Stadiou Street, Athens 00000 or calling 01/323.6962; telex: 214269 XEPE GR; fax: 01/322.5449; Postal address: XENEPEL.

For reservations while in Athens: Karageorgis Servias and 2 Stadiou Street (inside the National Bank of Greece branch), tel.: 01/323.7193. Open Monday through Friday from 08.00 - 20.00 and Saturdays from 08.00 - 14.00. You can also find rooms through the Tourist Police office in Mykonos.

How to get around

Buses serve the main villages and the most popular beaches on the following routes from the Hora: Ano Mera-Kalafatis-Elias/Tourlos- Agios Stefanos/Ornos-Agios Ioannis/Psarou-Platys Yialos/Airport.

Caiques (summer only) leave from Platys Yialos for the best beaches in the south and from the Hora for Super Paradise and Elia.

Taxis serve those parts of the island where the roads are passable.

And you can hire a car or motorbike from the numerous rental agencies in the Hora.

Tours are also organized by the island's many travel agencies, which are listed here with their telephone numbers:
Aegean Travel, 23.284
Mykonos Travel, 22.232
Bank Travel, 24.402
Veronis Agency, 22.687
Aris Yiannakakis Travel, 22.089
Delia Travel, 22.322
Ecotourism Travel, 24.415
Eros Travel, 22.312
Ellenis Travel, 23.910
Kousathanas Travel, 22.242
M.S. Enterprise, 24.459
Meridian Mykonos Travel, 24.702
Mykonos Accommodation Center, 23.160
Mykonos International, 24.653
Paralos, 22.227
Sun Spots Travel, 24.630
Sea and Sky Travel, 22.853
GATS Mykonos, 22.404
Holiday Plans, 22.233

Eating and entertainment

It is no exaggeration to say that Mykonos has everything in this line. There are restaurants of all kinds, to suit every taste and every pocketbook, from fast food joints, restaurants serving international cuisine, tavernas serving traditional Greek food, fish tavernas, ouzeries, discos, nightclubs, bars, pubs, cafes and sweet shops. In the evening the Hora gives the impression of being one big discotheque. Everyone gathers in its narrow, lit up lanes that reverberate with the sounds of music.

The revelry lasts until the wee hours of the morning. Only then will the late-nighters sleep, to awake around noon and spill out onto the island's countless beaches.

Sports

Mykonos offers mainly sports connected with the sea, such as swimming, waterskiing, windsurfing and sailing.

Food and other supplies

You can buy dry goods from the grocery stores in the Hora and Ano Mera, meat from the Hora's butchers, delicious bread and rusks from the bakers in the

Hora and Ano Mera, vegetables from the green grocers or picturesque strolling vendors, newspapers and magazines from the two news agents in the Hora. You can also buy fresh fish since the surrounding sea is a rich fishing ground.

Local specialties

Mykonos produces many kinds of cheese; try the fresh "tyrovolia", piquant "kopanisti" and others. "Melopittes" (small tarts made of dough, honey and tyrovolia), sausages made of pork and aromatic greens, "louza" (smoked pork) and "lardi" (salt pork), "amygdalota" (sweets made of crushed almonds) and "soumada" (a drink made from crushed almonds) are other Mykonian delicacies.

Shopping

You'll find boutiques specializing in fur and gold jewelry, folk arts and crafts, souvenirs (wooden boat models, windmills, watercolours inspired by the island), leatherwork (sandals, belts, bags), ceramics and lots of handmade fabrics.

Miscellaneous information

The OTE (Greek Telephone Company) has offices in the Hora where you can make calls and send telegrams anywhere in the world.
Opening hours: from October - 15 June, 07.30 - 22.00; 16 June - end September, 07.30 - 24.00. Closed on weekends.
Post Office (ELTA): 22.238
Taxi rank: 23.700, 22.400
Health Centre: 23.994-7
Bank, pharmacists and doctors are also to be found in the Hora.
There are six auto repairshops and three gasoline stations (two on the road between the Hora and Ano Mera, one on the road to Platys Yialos).
You should also be aware of Greece's official holidays, which in addition to the moveable feasts of Easter, Clean Monday (beginning of Lent) and

Whitmonday are as follows:

Jan.	Mar.	May.	Aug.	Oct.	Dec.
1, 6	25	1	15	28	25

Banking hours are: Monday through Thursday, 08.00 - 14.00, and Friday, 08.00 - 13.30.
Petrol stations are open from 07.00 - 19.00 daily, 07.00 - 15.00 Saturdays, and there is always one on duty round the clock and on Sundays.
Pharmacists keep regular shop hours during the week and on weekends and holidays, shops stay open on a rotating basis.
It is also important to remember that spending the night in Delos is not permitted.

Useful Telephone Numbers

Mykonos
Area Code: 0289
Police: 22.235
Tourist Police: 22.482
Mykonos Town Hall: 22.201
Municipal Office of the Press and Information: 23.990
Olympic Airlines (Ticket Office): 22.490
Olympic Airlines (Airport): 22.327
Port Authority: 22.218
Customs: 22.492
Bus Station (KTEL): 23.360
Archaeological Museum: 22.325
Folk Art Museum: 22.591
Maritime Museum of the Aegean: 22.700

Delos
OTE: 22.259
Archaeological Museum: 22.259
French Archaeological School: 23.738

CLASS	NAME/PLACE	TEL.	ROOMS	BEDS
	Agia Anna			
B	Anastasia (B)	71205	28	56
	Agios Stefanos			
A	Princess of Mykonos (P)	23806	13	25
B	Alkistis (B)	22332	102	182
C	Artemis	22345	23	39
C	Panorama	22337	27	51
D	Mina	23024	15	28
	Ano Mera			
A	Ano Mera	71230	67	124
	Hora			
A	Cavo Tagoo	23692	25	47
A	Leto	22207	25	48
B	Anastassios-Sevasti	22876	30	56
B	Calypso	23415	31	58
B	Despotiko	22009	21	40
B	Glastros (P)	23453	13	26
B	Ilio Maris (Despotika)	23755	22	41
B	Kouneni (Tria Pigadia)	22301	19	36
B	Kyma (Angelika)	23415	31	59
B	Les Moulins (P)	23240	14	25
B	Mykonos Bay (Megali Ammos)	23338	31	62
B	Petassos	22608	16	31
B	Poseidon A	22437	21	40
B	Poseidon B	22437	20	36
B	Rohari	23107	53	99
B	Theoxenia	22230	57	93
B	Vassiliou (P)	-	13	24
C	Adonis	22434	14	27
C	Aegaeon (B)	22869	28	47
C	Aeolos	23535	25	48
C	Bellou (Megali Ammos)	22589	7	14
C	Elysium (H&B)	23952	39	72
C	Gorgona	24544	17	33
C	Korfos	22850	18	42
C	Manoula's Beach (Ag. Ioannis-Diakofti)	22900	30	57
C	Manto	22330	15	26
C	Marianna	22072	23	43
C	Marios	22704	14	26
C	Matoyanni	22217	15	29
C	Mykonos (Vida)	22434	15	30
C	Mykonos Beach (B) (Megali Ammos)	22572	27	50
C	Niochori (F.A.)	-	5	9
C	Pelecan	23454	23	44
C	Thea Paradissou	24636	14	26
C	Thomas (Hondros Gremos)	23148	38	76
C	Vencia	23665	32	60
C	Zannis	22486	19	36
C	Zelyros	23928	29	56
C	Zorzis	22167	10	20
D	Apollon	22223	20	33
D	Delfines	22292	7	14
D	Delos	22312	8	16
D	Drafaki	22116	13	26
D	Helena	22361	21	41
D	Karbonaki (Fournakia)	23127	21	39
D	Karbonis	22217	9	17
D	Maria (Limni)	24212	10	20
D	Markos Beach	22811	11	23
D	Myconian Inn	22663	10	20
D	Nazos	22626	14	26
D	Omiros (Tagoo)	23328	10	20
D	Philippi	22294	13	27
D	Spanelis (Tagoo)	23081	11	20
E	Alekos (Laka)	-	9	18
E	Damianos (Drossopezoula)	23085	17	34

CLASS	NAME/PLACE	TEL.	ROOMS	BEDS
E	Galini (Laka)	22065	7	14
E	Gryparis (Dexamenes)	23463	15	21
E	Gyzi (Hondros Gremos)	23511	9	18
E	Iasson	23481	13	26
E	Ibiscus	23389	10	20
E	Kastelakia	22571	9	18
E	Lefteris	23128	8	14
E	Loucas	23489	11	20
E	Madalena	22954	28	51
E	Matina	22387	14	28
E	Milena (Drafaki)	23126	9	19
E	Olympia	22964	7	14
E	Psarrou Beach	22382	25	48
E	Tagoo	22611	20	37
E	Vangelis	22458	8	16
	Kalafatis			
B	Afroditi (B)	71367	135	256
	Ornos			
A	Santa Marina (F.A.)	23220	10	18
A	Santa Marina III (F.A.)	23220	3	6
A	Petinos Beach(H&B)	24310	14	25
B	Ornos Bay (P)	23961	15	29
B	Ornos Beach	22243	24	42
C	Glaros	23734	22	41
C	Paralos Beach	22600	40	76
C	Pigal	22825	6	11
C	Santa Marina II (F.A.)	23220	8	13
C	Skios	22470	13	26
C	Xydakis	-	33	62
C	Yannaki	23393	39	75
D	Asteri	22715	13	24
D	Meltemi	23134	14	23
D	Santa Marina I	23220	9	13
E	Anixi	23561	15	31
E	Costas	23090	8	20
E	Eleftheria	23092	7	14
E	Eva	23403	16	32
	Platys Yialos			
	Petassos Bay (B)	23737	21	40
B	Petassos Beach	23437	64	128
C	Kamari	23424	35	67
C	Petinos	23680	29	57
D	Akti	23982	11	19
D	Nissaki	22913	14	26
D	Platys Yialos Beach	22913	11	19
E	Aktoyiali	22125	22	41
E	Anna	22221	9	19
F	Argo	22127	14	26
E	Neraida	22093	8	16
	Tourlos			
B	Irini Tourlos Beach (P)	22306	14	27
B	Olia	23823	27	51
B	Rinia (B)	22300	37	70
C	Monoyios (F.A.)	-	7	14
D	Alex	23030	10	20
D	Iliovassilema	23013	17	36
	Vrissi			
B	Kohili	22107	29	55
B	Viennoula's Garden	22983	21	36
C	Korali	22929	28	54
C	Mangas	22577	19	37
D	Karrop Tree	22038	18	36
D	Madoupas	23729	16	19
E	Sourmeli Garden	22905	10	19

Note: B=Bungalows, F.A.=Furnished Apartments, H&B=Hotel & Bungalows, P=Pension